EXTREME WEATHER JOBS

SMOKEJUMPERS

BY ASHLEY GISH

WWW.APEXEDITIONS.COM

Apex is distributed by North Star Editions:
sales@northstareditions.com | 888-417-0195

Produced for Apex by Red Line Editorial.

Photographs ©: Elaine Thompson/AP Images, cover, 20; Carrie Bilbao/BLM/National Interagency Fire Center, 1, 26–27; Shutterstock Images, 4–5, 12, 14–15, 24; Mitch Hanson/BLM/National Interagency Fire Center, 6–7; iStockphoto, 8, 9, 16–17, 22–23; US Forest Service, 10–11, 13, 29; Neal Herbert/DOI/National Interagency Fire Center, 18; Chad Harder/AP Images, 19; NIFC/BLM, 25

Library of Congress Control Number: 2023921614

ISBN
978-1-63738-919-5 (hardcover)
978-1-63738-959-1 (paperback)
979-8-89250-055-5 (ebook pdf)
979-8-89250-017-3 (hosted ebook)

Printed in the United States of America
Mankato, MN
082024

NOTE TO PARENTS AND EDUCATORS

Apex books are designed to build literacy skills in striving readers. Exciting, high-interest content attracts and holds readers' attention. The text is carefully leveled to allow students to achieve success quickly. Additional features, such as bolded glossary words for difficult terms, help build comprehension.

CHAPTER 1
DROPPING IN 4

CHAPTER 2
HISTORY 10

CHAPTER 3
TOUGH TRAINING 16

CHAPTER 4
HARD AT WORK 22

COMPREHENSION QUESTIONS • 28
GLOSSARY • 30
TO LEARN MORE • 31
ABOUT THE AUTHOR • 31
INDEX • 32

DROPPING IN

An airplane flies over a wildfire. Smoke hides the ground below. But a team of smokejumpers is ready to help.

Wildfires can burn huge areas of land. They send thick clouds of smoke high into the air.

The airplane flies to the edge of the fire. Then, the smokejumpers leap out. They **deploy** their parachutes and drift to the ground.

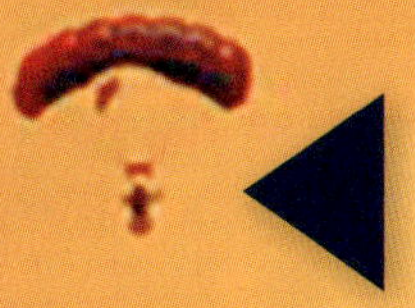

Smokejumpers parachute into an area called the hot zone.

FAST FACT

Smokejumpers may leap from planes flying 3,000 feet (900 m) above the ground.

Smokejumpers may use chainsaws to cut through large tree trunks.

The smokejumpers quickly dig a **fire line**. They use axes to chop down trees. They use shovels to clear small branches. Without fuel to burn, the fire starts to die out.

FIRST FIGHTERS

Smokejumpers fly to wildfires in **remote** locations. It takes a long time to drive to these places. But smokejumpers arrive quickly. They stop fires from spreading while other firefighters are on the way.

Smokejumpers work in places where fire trucks can't easily reach.

CHAPTER 2

Firefighters first practiced parachuting from airplanes in the 1930s. Before this, reaching fires in remote areas was nearly impossible.

Francis Lufkin practiced parachute jumping in 1939. He went on to become one of the first smokejumpers.

The Nez Perce National Forest is in Idaho.

The first fire jump happened in 1940. It took place in the Nez Perce National Forest. The jump was a success. Soon after, other places started creating smokejumper teams.

STAYING SAFE

Early smokejumping was very risky. Jumpers could get hurt if they crashed or ran into trees. But people invented better **equipment**. They made parachutes easier to steer. And they made tough suits for smokejumpers to wear.

Early smokejumpers worked to create parachutes that let them land safely in rough areas.

Russia has nearly 2 billion acres (800 million ha) of forests.

By 2023, there were nine smokejumper bases in the United States. Russia and Canada had smokejumpers, too.

FAST FACT

Russia has more smokejumpers than any other country.

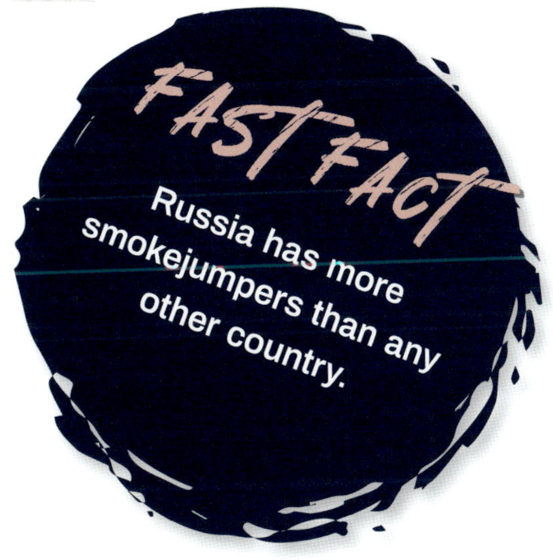

CHAPTER 3

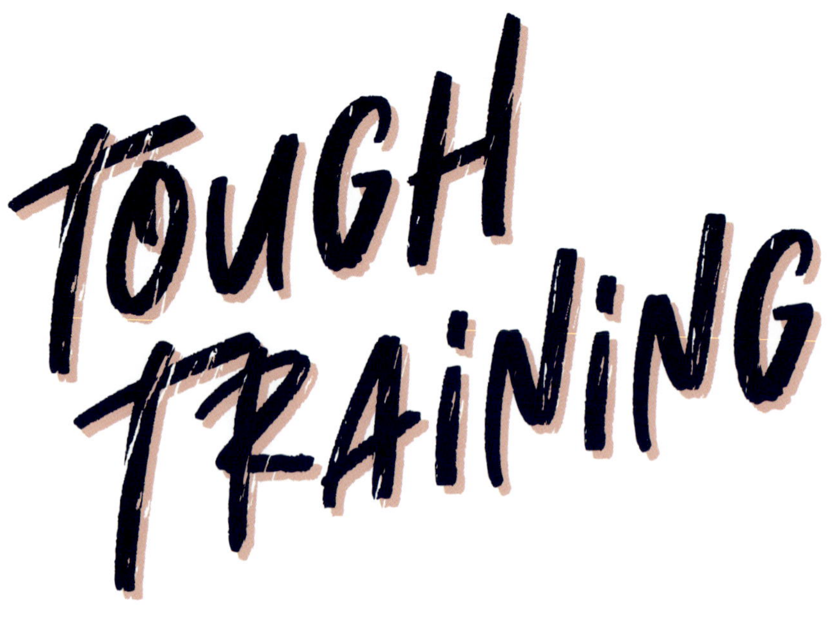

TOUGH TRAINING

Only **experienced** firefighters can become smokejumpers. They train for weeks. First, they do **physical** tests. They must run fast and far while carrying heavy gear.

Firefighters must be in shape to become smokejumpers.

Then smokejumpers practice skydiving. They learn how to use and fix parachutes. They practice jumping and landing safely.

Smokejumpers pull cords to steer parachutes through changing winds.

Smokejumpers train to climb up and down trees. That way, they are prepared in case parachutes get caught.

TREE LANDINGS

Sometimes smokejumpers land in trees. They use ropes to get down safely. They tie one end of each rope to the tree. The other end clips to a smokejumper's harness.

Part of smokejumpers' training includes falling off a tall tower. Trainees are attached to a cable for safety. They learn how to fall so they don't get hurt.

◀ **Trainees fall from the tower at up to 15 miles per hour (24 km/h).**

CHAPTER 4

HARD AT WORK

Wildfire season goes from spring until fall. Smokejumpers may be called to work at any time during this season. They gear up and fly out from their bases.

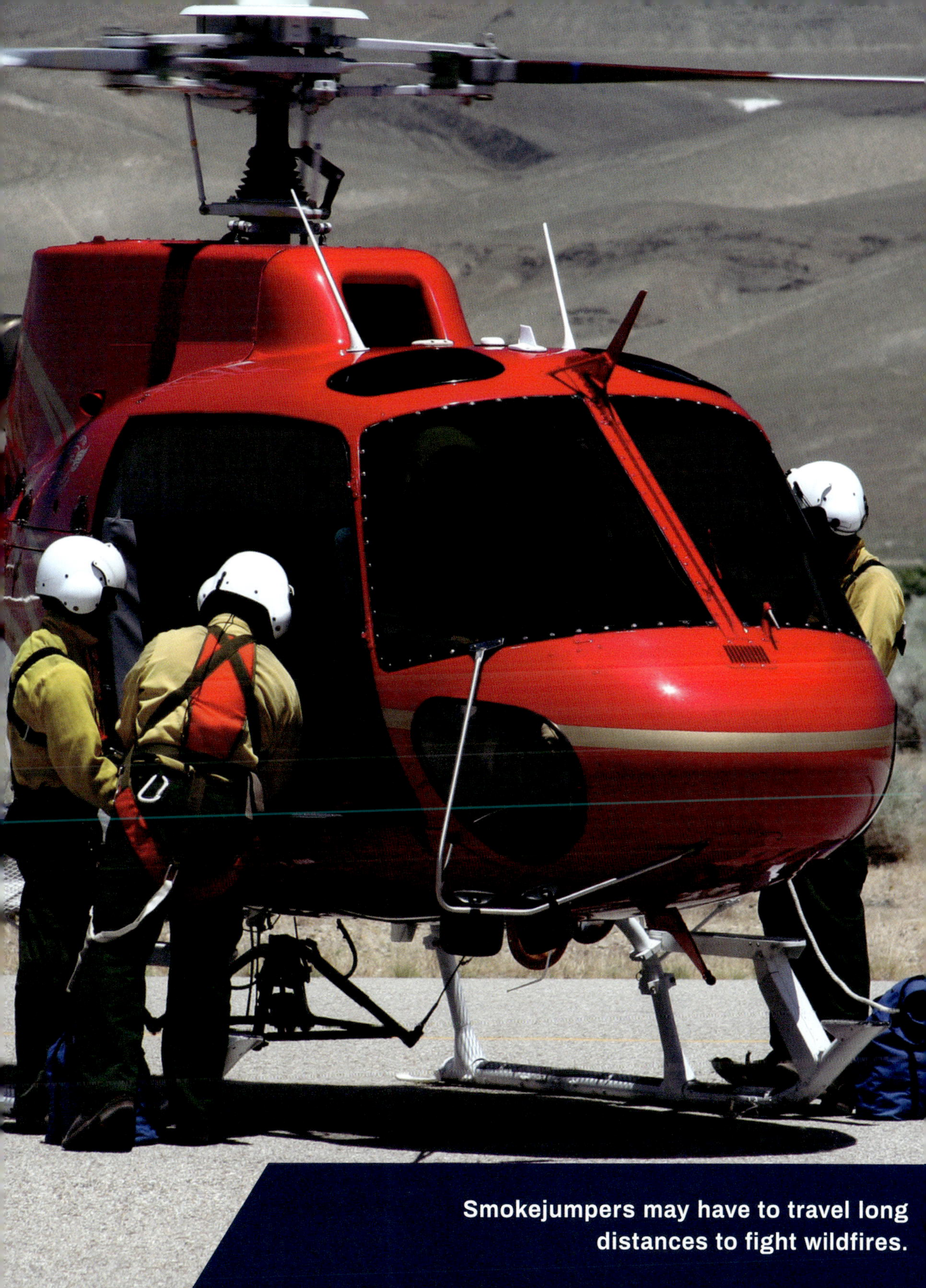

Smokejumpers may have to travel long distances to fight wildfires.

Smokejumpers land near a wildfire. Then they plan how to stop it. They clear away **flammable** brush. They also dig **trenches** in front of the fire.

Smokejumpers may spend up to 16 hours a day digging trenches to slow wildfires.

Smokejumpers carry packs that can weigh up to 100 pounds (45 kg).

SUPPLIES

Smokejumpers may be out working for many days. Planes drop some supplies. But smokejumpers carry many with them. They haul food, water, axes, and shovels.

Fighting wildfires is very **dangerous**. So, smokejumpers wear safety gear. Helmets protect their heads. Padded jumpsuits protect their bodies from flames and hard falls.

A smokejumper's helmet has a cage at the front. This part protects the person's face.

COMPREHENSION QUESTIONS

Write your answers on a separate piece of paper.

1. Write a few sentences describing the main ideas of Chapter 2.

2. Would you want to work as a smokejumper? Why or why not?

3. From what height might smokejumpers jump out of airplanes?

- **A.** 2,000 feet (600 m)
- **B.** 3,000 feet (900 m)
- **C.** 5,000 feet (1,500 m)

4. Why would a parachute that is easier to steer be safer for smokejumpers?

- **A.** They could fall slower.
- **B.** They could fall faster.
- **C.** They could avoid trees and rocks.

5. What does **risky** mean in this book?

Early smokejumping was very ***risky****. Jumpers could get hurt if they crashed or ran into trees.*

A. full of danger
B. safe and easy
C. costing lots of money

6. What does **trainees** mean in this book?

Part of smokejumpers' training includes falling off a tall tower. ***Trainees*** *are attached to a cable for safety.*

A. people who are in training
B. places where training happens
C. times when training happens

Answer key on page 32.

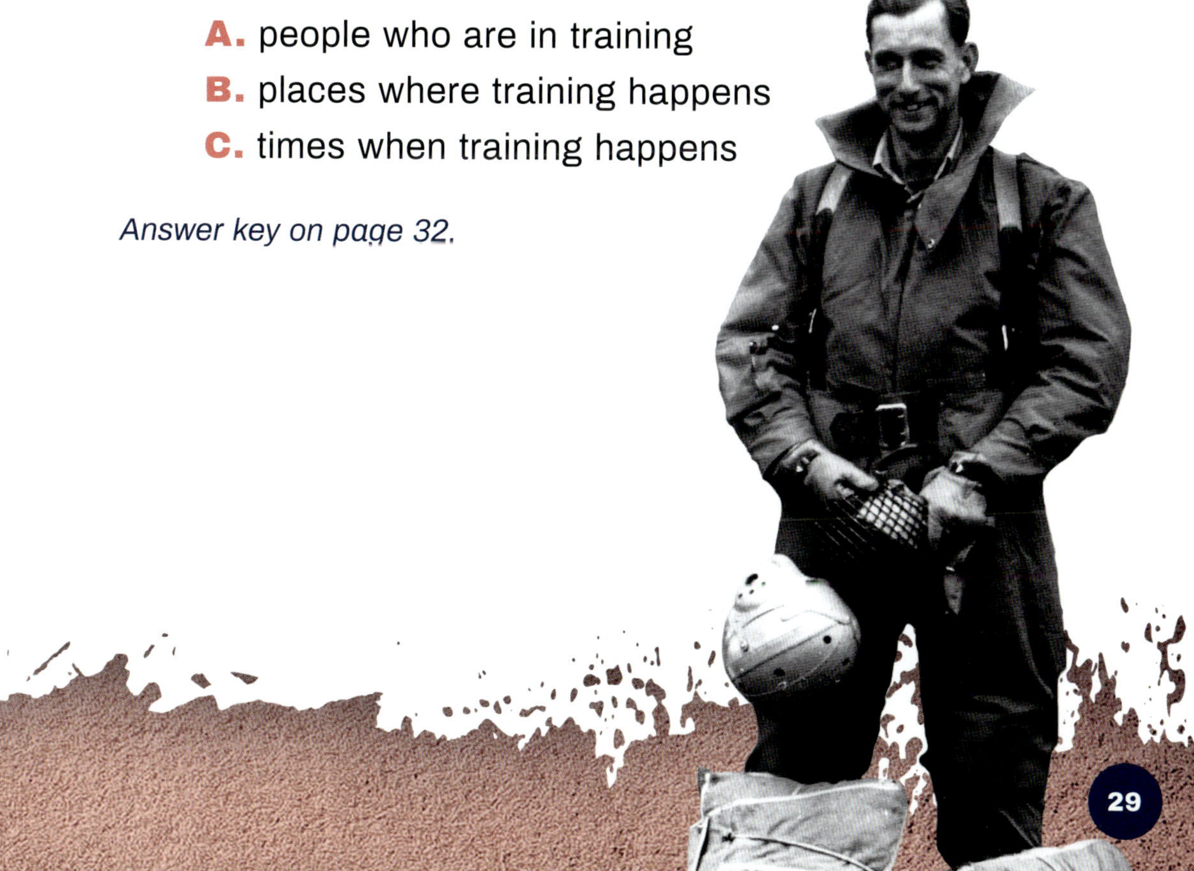

GLOSSARY

dangerous

Likely to cause problems or harm.

deploy

To use something.

equipment

Tools or machines used to do a job.

experienced

Having skills or knowledge in something as a result of doing it before.

fire line

A strip of land that has been cleared of things that can burn.

flammable

Able to catch fire easily.

physical

Involving speed, strength, or quick movements.

remote

Far away from towns or people.

trenches

Long, narrow ditches dug into the ground.

TO LEARN MORE

BOOKS

Bell, Samantha S. *Smokejumper: 12 Things to Know*. Mankato, MN: 12-Story Library, 2021.

Murray, Julie. *Smokejumpers*. Minneapolis: Abdo Publishing, 2021.

Ransom, Candice. *Wildfires*. Mendota Heights, MN: Apex Editions, 2023.

ONLINE RESOURCES

Visit **www.apexeditions.com** to find links and resources related to this title.

ABOUT THE AUTHOR

Ashley Gish has authored more than 60 juvenile nonfiction books. She lives in Minnesota.

INDEX

A

axes, 8, 25

C

cable, 21
Canada, 15

E

equipment, 13

F

fuel, 8

H

harness, 19
helmets, 26

J

jumpsuits, 26

N

Nez Perce National Forest, 12

P

parachutes, 6, 10, 13, 18

R

rope, 19
Russia, 15

S

shovels, 8, 25
skydiving, 18

T

trainees, 21
trenches, 24

U

United States, 15

ANSWER KEY:
1. Answers will vary; 2. Answers will vary; 3. B; 4. C; 5. A; 6. A